W9-CFV-542

ANIMAL DETECTIVES

MILITARY DOLPHINS

Rosie Albright

PowerKiDS
press™

New York

Published in 2012 by The Rosen Publishing Group, Inc.
29 East 21st Street, New York, NY 10010

First Edition

Editor: Joanne Randolph
Designer: Kate Laczynski

Photo Credits: Cover, pp. 10, 12–13, 17, 24 (bite plate, handler) © Louise Murray/age fotostock; pp. 5, 14, 18 Shutterstock.com; p. 6 © www.iStockphoto.com/Alexey Tkachenko; p. 9 Brien Aho/U.S. Navy/Getty Images; pp. 21, 24 (waterway) Frank Rossoto Stocktrek/Getty Images; p. 22 U.S. Navy/Getty Images.

Library of Congress Cataloging-in-Publication Data

Albright, Rosie.
  Military dolphins / by Rosie Albright. — 1st ed.
      p. cm. — (Animal detectives)
  Includes index.
  ISBN 978-1-4488-6153-8 (library binding) — ISBN 978-1-4488-6258-0 (pbk.) — ISBN 978-1-4488-6259-7 (6-pack)
  1. Bottlenose dolphin—War use—Juvenile literature. 2. United States. Navy—Juvenile literature. I. Title.
  UH100.5.B68A43 2012
  359.4'24—dc23
                              2011022767

Manufactured in the United States of America

CPSIA Compliance Information: Batch #WW12PK: For Further Information contact Rosen Publishing, New York, New York at 1-800-237-9932

CONTENTS

Dolphins are smart. They are easy to train, too.

Dolphins are trained using food. When they learn new skills, they get fish.

The Navy and Marines train dolphins. The trained dolphins are called military dolphins.

The person who trains a military dolphin is its **handler**.

Military dolphins are trained in San Diego, California. The dolphins live in special pens.

Military dolphins look for mines in the water. They use special tools to mark the mines.

Dolphins hold most tools with their mouths. The part they hold is called the **bite plate**.

17

Military dolphins look for enemy swimmers, too. Then naval officers can stop them from hurting people.

Dolphins keep **waterways** safe during wars. Supplies can get to people who need them.

Military dolphins have been used in the war in Iraq. They have saved many lives.

WORDS TO KNOW

bite plate

handler

waterway

INDEX

WEB SITES

Due to the changing nature of Internet links, PowerKids Press has developed an online list of Web sites related to the subject of this book. This site is updated regularly. Please use this link to access the list:

www.powerkidslinks.com/andt/dolphin